Workbook

companion to

Divorced.
Catholic.
Now What?

Navigating Your Life After Divorce

by Lisa Duffy and Vince Frese

A Journey of Hope Publication

Journey of Hope Productions
12460 Crabapple Road
Suite 202 Box 113
Alpharetta, GA 30004

ISBN 978-0-9718234-2-6

Chapter One:

Praying in Times of Distress

1 | Chapter One:
Praying in Times of Distress

Reflection Questions:

On a scale of 1 - 10, 10 being the best, how would I rate my ability to pray right now? To what do I attribute this to?

_____

_____

_____

_____

_____

_____

_____

_____

_____

_____

_____

_____

_____

When I think of the word "prayer" what is my initial reaction to it? You may understand that prayer is necessary, but what response does that word bring in your heart? Peace? Depression? Consolation? Guilt? What do think the cause of this emotion is?

_____

_____

_____

_____

_____

_____

_____

_____

_____

_____

_____

_____

_____

After reading this chapter, which form of prayer would I like to try and why?

_____

_____

_____

_____

_____

_____

_____

_____

_____

_____

_____

_____

_____

_____

_____

Meditation Notes

_____

_____

_____

_____

_____

_____

_____

_____

Other Insights or Inspirations

_____

_____

_____

_____

_____

_____

Journaling

_____

_____

_____

_____

_____

_____

_____

_____

_____

_____

_____

_____

_____

_____

_____

_____

_____

Journaling

_____

_____

_____

_____

_____

_____

_____

_____

_____

_____

_____

_____

_____

_____

_____

_____

_____

Journaling

_____

_____

_____

_____

_____

_____

_____

_____

_____

_____

_____

_____

_____

_____

_____

_____

_____

Chapter Two:

Anger with Your Spouse, Yourself, and with God

2 | Chapter Two:
Anger with Your Spouse, Yourself,
and with God

Reflection Questions:

At whom, or at what are you directing your anger right now, and why?

_____

_____

_____

_____

_____

_____

_____

_____

_____

_____

_____

_____

_____

_____

Do you feel that you are not angry right now, that the primary emotion you feel toward your ex-spouse is pity?

_____

_____

_____

_____

_____

_____

_____

_____

_____

_____

_____

_____

_____

_____

_____

_____

_____

Do you feel in control of your anger and your emotions in general, or do you feel they are out of control? Why?

_____

_____

_____

_____

_____

_____

_____

_____

_____

_____

_____

_____

_____

_____

_____

_____

Now What?

Write down the action point you chose to use and the result of your action.

The point I chose to use was:

_____

_____

The result of my action was:

_____

_____

_____

_____

_____

_____

_____

_____

Do I feel this helped me in my situation?

_____

_____

_____

_____

Implementation Questions

Are you finding it easy or difficult to include God in your life and talk to him about the way you feel? How seriously do you believe that God can help you through this situation?

_____

_____

_____

_____

_____

_____

_____

Suppressing your anger is not healthy, nor is expressing it in a destructive or a negatively aggressive manner. Make a list of some constructive ways to channel your anger.

_____

_____

_____

_____

_____

Meditation Notes

_____

_____

_____

_____

_____

_____

_____

_____

_____

Other Insights or Inspirations

_____

_____

_____

_____

_____

_____

_____

Journaling

_____

_____

_____

_____

_____

_____

_____

_____

_____

_____

_____

_____

_____

_____

_____

_____

_____

_____

Journaling

_____

_____

_____

_____

_____

_____

_____

_____

_____

_____

_____

_____

_____

_____

_____

_____

_____

_____

Journaling

_____

_____

_____

_____

_____

_____

_____

_____

_____

_____

_____

_____

_____

_____

_____

_____

Chapter Three:

Why Did God Allow This to Happen to Me?

3 | Chapter Three:
Why Did God Allow This to Happen to Me?

Reflection Questions:

What is your perspective on this? Do you believe God has a plan?

_____

_____

_____

_____

_____

_____

_____

_____

_____

_____

_____

_____

_____

_____

_____

_____

If you believe that God does have a plan, how has that shed light on your own situation?

_____

_____

_____

_____

_____

_____

_____

_____

_____

_____

_____

_____

_____

_____

_____

Are you finding hope is something easy or difficult to identify with now?

_____

_____

_____

_____

_____

_____

_____

_____

_____

_____

_____

_____

_____

_____

Now What?

Write down the action point you chose to use and the result of your action.

The point I chose to use was:

_____

_____

The result of my action was:

_____

_____

_____

_____

_____

_____

_____

Do I feel this helped me in my situation?

_____

_____

_____

_____

Goals Chart

Tomorrow	Next Year	In 3 Years	In 5 Years

Implementation Questions

Am I able to see some positives in my circumstances? What are they?

_____

_____

_____

_____

What would I say is my biggest challenge right now?

_____

_____

_____

_____

In the every day circumstances of my life, especially in regard to my relationship with my former spouse, is it possible to see a bigger reason for what is happening?

_____

_____

_____

_____

_____

_____

Meditation Notes

_____

_____

_____

_____

_____

_____

_____

_____

Other Insights or Inspirations

_____

_____

_____

_____

_____

_____

Journaling

_____

_____

_____

_____

_____

_____

_____

_____

_____

_____

_____

_____

_____

_____

_____

_____

_____

Journaling

_____

_____

_____

_____

_____

_____

_____

_____

_____

_____

_____

_____

_____

_____

_____

_____

_____

Journaling

_____

_____

_____

_____

_____

_____

_____

_____

_____

_____

_____

_____

_____

_____

_____

_____

_____

Journaling

_____

_____

_____

_____

_____

_____

_____

_____

_____

_____

_____

_____

_____

_____

_____

_____

_____

_____

Chapter Four:

What Does the Church Really Teach About Divorce?

4 | Chapter Four:
What Does the Church Really Teach About Divorce?

Reflection Questions:

What is your perspective on the statements made by John, Linda, and David in the book? Have you heard any of these same things?

_____

_____

_____

_____

_____

_____

_____

_____

_____

_____

_____

_____

_____

_____

Do you find it difficult or easy to attend mass or go to parish functions since your divorce?

_____

_____

_____

_____

_____

_____

_____

_____

_____

_____

_____

_____

_____

_____

What are some questions you may have about this issue that you would like to find the answers to?

_____

_____

_____

_____

_____

_____

_____

_____

_____

_____

_____

_____

_____

_____

_____

Now What?

Write down the action point you chose to use and the result of your action.

The point I chose to use was:

_____

_____

The result of my action was:

_____

_____

_____

_____

_____

_____

_____

_____

Do I feel this helped me in my situation?

_____

_____

_____

_____

Implementation Questions

Do I believe that I have been completely honest with myself about what happened in my marriage?

_____

_____

_____

_____

Have I considered talking to my spouse about reconciling? Why or why not?

_____

_____

_____

_____

After reading this chapter, do I understand where I stand with Christ and the Church?

_____

_____

_____

_____

_____

Meditation Notes

_____

_____

_____

_____

_____

_____

_____

_____

_____

Other Insights or Inspirations

_____

_____

_____

_____

_____

_____

_____

Journaling

_____

_____

_____

_____

_____

_____

_____

_____

_____

_____

_____

_____

_____

_____

_____

_____

_____

Journaling

_____

_____

_____

_____

_____

_____

_____

_____

_____

_____

_____

_____

_____

_____

_____

_____

_____

Journaling

_____

_____

_____

_____

_____

_____

_____

_____

_____

_____

_____

_____

_____

_____

_____

_____

_____

_____

_____

Chapter Five:

What Is an Annulment?

5 | Chapter Five:
What Is an Annulment?

Reflection Questions:

What is your own opinion about the annulment process? Have you heard any of these same things?

_____

_____

_____

_____

_____

_____

_____

_____

_____

_____

_____

_____

_____

_____

_____

At this point in time do you have an interest in going through the annulment process? Why or why not?

_____

_____

_____

_____

_____

_____

_____

_____

_____

_____

_____

_____

_____

_____

_____

_____

What are the comments I have heard other people say about the annulment process? Am I likely to believe that my experience will be similar to theirs?

_____

_____

_____

_____

_____

_____

_____

_____

_____

_____

_____

_____

_____

_____

Now What?

Write down the action point you chose to use and the result of your action.

The point I chose to use was:

_____

_____

The result of my action was:

_____

_____

_____

_____

_____

_____

_____

_____

Do I feel this helped me in my situation?

_____

_____

_____

_____

Implementation Questions

In my own words, can I describe how the annulment process might bring healing into my life? Do I feel that I will be open to remarrying in the future? Why or why not?

_____

_____

_____

_____

_____

_____

After reading this chapter, do I have a better understanding of what the annulment process is?

_____

_____

_____

_____

_____

_____

_____

Meditation Notes

_____

_____

_____

_____

_____

_____

_____

_____

_____

Other Insights or Inspirations

_____

_____

_____

_____

_____

_____

_____

Annulment Preparation Worksheet

Before you begin the process it is a good idea to be aware of the different types of information you will need to have readily available. Check off each corresponding box for the information you can provide and then find out how you can obtain those whose boxes you cannot check.

- ☐ A complete and correct mailing address for your former spouse, or a letter detailing your efforts to locate your former spouse.
- ☐ Your Marriage License or Marriage Certificate.
- ☐ Your Divorce Decree.
- ☐ Baptismal Certificates of the Catholic spouse(s).
- ☐ Complete names and mailing addresses for at least four witnesses.

It is a good idea to make and keep a photocopy of everything you submit to the Tribunal, in case there are problems with mailing. Think carefully about who you would ask to be your witnesses. The best witness would be someone who witnessed your marriage and knew you and your spouse while you dated. If you don't have anyone close to you in that way, someone who knew you as a couple – more than the average person knew you – Make a preliminary list of who you might ask:

_____

_____

_____

What are the primary reasons you believe you may have a case?

_____

_____

_____

_____

Journaling

_____

_____

_____

_____

_____

_____

_____

_____

_____

_____

_____

_____

_____

_____

_____

_____

_____

Journaling

_____

_____

_____

_____

_____

_____

_____

_____

_____

_____

_____

_____

_____

_____

_____

_____

_____

Chapter Six:

Stay Close to the Sacraments

6 | Chapter Six:
Stay Close to the Sacraments

Reflection Questions:

Have I found receiving the sacraments to be of help during this difficult time?

_____

_____

_____

_____

_____

_____

_____

_____

_____

_____

_____

_____

_____

_____

What was my sacramental life like before my divorce? Has it improved or has it lapsed?

_____

_____

_____

_____

_____

_____

_____

_____

_____

_____

_____

_____

_____

_____

_____

_____

_____

Can I relate at all to Cathy's story?

_____

_____

_____

_____

_____

_____

_____

_____

_____

_____

_____

_____

_____

_____

_____

Now What?

Write down the action point you chose to use and the result of your action.

The point I chose to use was:

_____

_____

The result of my action was:

_____

_____

_____

_____

_____

_____

_____

Do I feel this helped me in my situation?

_____

_____

_____

_____

Implementation Questions

Am I able to see the benefits of going to confession frequently or is it difficult for me to feel comfortable about going?

_____

_____

_____

_____

_____

_____

Can I recall a time when receiving the sacraments affected a change in my life?

_____

_____

_____

_____

_____

Meditation Notes

_____

_____

_____

_____

_____

_____

_____

_____

Other Insights or Inspirations

_____

_____

_____

_____

_____

_____

_____

Journaling

_____

_____

_____

_____

_____

_____

_____

_____

_____

_____

_____

_____

_____

_____

_____

_____

_____

_____

Journaling

Journaling

_____

_____

_____

_____

_____

_____

_____

_____

_____

_____

_____

_____

_____

_____

_____

_____

_____

_____

Chapter Seven:

Dealing With the Ex-Spouse

7 | Chapter Seven: Dealing With the Ex-Spouse

Reflection Questions:

Do I have a situation with my ex-spouse similar to the one Jill has described with hers?

_____

_____

_____

_____

_____

_____

_____

_____

_____

_____

_____

_____

_____

When I have to confront my ex-spouse, what are the things I fear will take place?

_____

_____

_____

_____

_____

_____

_____

_____

_____

_____

_____

_____

_____

_____

_____

_____

What is my typical reaction to a situation in which my ex-spouse is deliberately trying to upset me?

_____

_____

_____

_____

_____

_____

_____

_____

_____

_____

_____

_____

_____

_____

_____

_____

Now What?

Write down the action point you chose to use and the result of your action.

The point I chose to use was:

_____

_____

The result of my action was:

_____

_____

_____

_____

_____

_____

_____

_____

Do I feel this helped me in my situation?

_____

_____

_____

_____

Implementation Questions

How do I feel about treating my spouse in a charitable manner? Do I see it as something I can easily do or will it take a lot of work to get to that point?

_____

_____

_____

_____

_____

Am I able to see my ex-spouse as Christ does – precious and valuable – even though I have been through so much in my divorce? What are some concrete ways I can begin treating my ex-spouse in a loving manner?

_____

_____

_____

_____

_____

_____

_____

Meditation Notes

_____

_____

_____

_____

_____

_____

_____

Other Insights or Inspirations

_____

_____

_____

_____

_____

_____

Journaling

_____

_____

_____

_____

_____

_____

_____

_____

_____

_____

_____

_____

_____

_____

_____

_____

Journaling

_____

_____

_____

_____

_____

_____

_____

_____

_____

_____

_____

_____

_____

_____

_____

_____

_____

Journaling

_____

_____

_____

_____

_____

_____

_____

_____

_____

_____

_____

_____

_____

_____

_____

_____

_____

Chapter Eight:

How Are the Children?

8 | Chapter Eight:
How Are the Children?

Reflection Questions:

Do you have similar feelings to what Tanya has described?

_____

_____

_____

_____

_____

_____

_____

_____

_____

_____

_____

_____

_____

How have your children reacted to your situation?

Children are not all the same, and depending on their age and the family foundation they have had prior to the divorce, communicate differently. On a scale of 1 - 10, 10 being best, how would you rate your child's/children's ability to communicate during your divorce? Why?

_____

_____

_____

_____

_____

_____

_____

_____

_____

_____

_____

_____

_____

_____

_____

Now What?

Write down the action point you chose to use and the result of your action.

The point I chose to use was:

_____

_____

The result of my action was:

_____

_____

_____

_____

_____

_____

_____

Do I feel this helped me in my situation?

_____

_____

_____

_____

Implementation Questions

What particular challenges am I facing with my kids? Have I been abler to identify and take positive steps to support my children?

_____

_____

_____

_____

_____

_____

As a parent, what are the things I can see my child/children need the most from me? How able am I to give them what they need? Am I comfortable in trying to keep my children focused on their faith, or is it a source of suffering or frustration for me?

_____

_____

_____

_____

_____

Meditation Notes

_____

_____

_____

_____

_____

_____

_____

_____

_____

_____

Other Insights or Inspirations

_____

_____

_____

_____

_____

_____

_____

Journaling

_____

_____

_____

_____

_____

_____

_____

_____

_____

_____

_____

_____

_____

_____

_____

_____

_____

Journaling

_____

_____

_____

_____

_____

_____

_____

_____

_____

_____

_____

_____

_____

_____

_____

_____

_____

_____

Journaling

Chapter Nine:

The Healing Begins

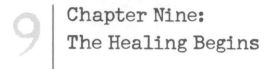

Chapter Nine:
The Healing Begins

Reflection Questions:

What are your thoughts on John's story?

_____

_____

_____

_____

_____

_____

_____

_____

_____

_____

_____

_____

_____

_____

_____

Have you had any similar experiences to his?

_____

_____

_____

_____

_____

_____

_____

_____

_____

_____

_____

_____

_____

_____

_____

_____

_____

_____

What are you finding to be the most challenging about your situation right now?

_____

_____

_____

_____

_____

_____

_____

_____

_____

_____

_____

_____

_____

_____

_____

Now What?

Write down the action point you chose to use and the result of your action.

The point I chose to use was:

_____

_____

The result of my action was:

_____

_____

_____

_____

_____

_____

_____

_____

Do I feel this helped me in my situation?

_____

_____

_____

_____

Implementation Questions

Have I ever recognized a time in my life when Christ cared for me as the Good Samaritan?

_____

_____

_____

_____

_____

_____

Does the analogy of the Church as "the inn" help my understanding of why I need to stay close to my faith during this difficult time? Do I attend church regularly now? Why or why not?

_____

_____

_____

_____

_____

Meditation Notes

_____

_____

_____

_____

_____

_____

_____

_____

_____

Other Insights or Inspirations

_____

_____

_____

_____

_____

_____

Journaling

_____

_____

_____

_____

_____

_____

_____

_____

_____

_____

_____

_____

_____

_____

_____

_____

_____

Journaling

_____

_____

_____

_____

_____

_____

_____

_____

_____

_____

_____

_____

_____

_____

_____

_____

Journaling

_____

_____

_____

_____

_____

_____

_____

_____

_____

_____

_____

_____

_____

_____

_____

_____

_____

_____

Chapter Ten:
Your Own Self-Worth

10 | Chapter Ten:
Your Own Self-Worth

Reflection Questions:

How do I feel about what Carl has described?

_____

_____

_____

_____

_____

_____

_____

_____

_____

_____

_____

_____

_____

_____

_____

Are there any particular areas where I feel lacking in worthiness?

_____

_____

_____

_____

_____

_____

_____

_____

_____

_____

_____

_____

_____

_____

_____

If my self-esteem is intact, what are some things that have helped me in this area?

_____

_____

_____

_____

_____

_____

_____

_____

_____

_____

_____

_____

_____

_____

Now What?

Write down the action point you chose to use and the result of your action.

The point I chose to use was:

_____

_____

The result of my action was:

_____

_____

_____

_____

_____

_____

_____

Do I feel this helped me in my situation?

_____

_____

_____

_____

Implementation Questions

Do I believe that I have a lot to offer others, whether it be friends, family or a future relationship? Why or why not?

_____

_____

_____

_____

_____

_____

What are some of my gifts/talents/strong points? Am I utilizing any of these right now? If not, are there some ways I can put them to use?

_____

_____

_____

_____

_____

_____

Meditation Notes

_____

_____

_____

_____

_____

_____

_____

_____

Other Insights or Inspirations

_____

_____

_____

_____

_____

_____

_____

Take Inventory

Family	Work	Community

Journaling

Journaling

_____

_____

_____

_____

_____

_____

_____

_____

_____

_____

_____

_____

_____

_____

_____

_____

_____

Chapter Eleven:

The Value of Suffering

11 | Chapter Eleven:
The Value of Suffering

Reflection Questions:

Are you familiar with the term "offering up suffering?" How would you describe it in your own words?

_____

_____

_____

_____

_____

_____

_____

_____

_____

_____

_____

_____

_____

_____

Do you find it easy or difficult to do this now, as you suffer through your divorce?

_____

_____

_____

_____

_____

_____

_____

_____

_____

_____

_____

_____

_____

_____

_____

Through our suffering, Christ offers us the opportunity to share in his redemptive suffering . . . what are your thoughts on this great gift?

_____

_____

_____

_____

_____

_____

_____

_____

_____

_____

_____

_____

_____

_____

_____

Now What?

Write down the action point you chose to use and the result of your action.

The point I chose to use was:

_____

_____

The result of my action was:

_____

_____

_____

_____

_____

_____

_____

Do I feel this helped me in my situation?

_____

_____

_____

_____

Implementation Questions

When I am enduring some particular suffering, what helps me get through it?

_____

_____

_____

_____

_____

Do I have any specific suffering right now, other than the obvious, that I can offer for others?

_____

_____

_____

_____

_____

Meditation Notes

_____

_____

_____

_____

_____

_____

_____

_____

Other Insights or Inspirations

_____

_____

_____

_____

_____

_____

Journaling

_____

_____

_____

_____

_____

_____

_____

_____

_____

_____

_____

_____

_____

_____

_____

_____

_____

_____

Journaling

Journaling

_____

_____

_____

_____

_____

_____

_____

_____

_____

_____

_____

_____

_____

_____

_____

_____

_____

_____

Chapter Twelve:

Letting Go

12 | Chapter Twelve: Letting Go

Reflection Questions:

Have you thought at all about letting go of your marriage relationship and if so, what are your thoughts about it?

_____

_____

_____

_____

_____

_____

_____

_____

_____

_____

_____

_____

_____

_____

At this time, do you find it impossible, difficult or not so bad to consider letting go?

What could the positive consequences of letting go be for you?

_____

_____

_____

_____

_____

_____

_____

_____

_____

_____

_____

_____

_____

_____

_____

_____

Now What?

Write down the action point you chose to use and the result of your action.

The point I chose to use was:

_____

_____

The result of my action was:

_____

_____

_____

_____

_____

_____

_____

Do I feel this helped me in my situation?

_____

_____

_____

_____

Implementation Questions

Do I trust God enough to give him the control of this part of my life and have faith that he will take care of everything?

_____

_____

_____

_____

_____

_____

_____

What are some other suggestions on how to begin the process of letting go?

_____

_____

_____

_____

_____

_____

Meditation Notes

_____

_____

_____

_____

_____

_____

_____

_____

Other Insights or Inspirations

_____

_____

_____

_____

_____

_____

Questions for Reflection

Am I fearful when I think about the future alone? Why or why not?

_____

_____

Is it hard for me to admit that my marriage failed? Why? Is it pride?

_____

_____

Do I feel guilty because my marriage failed?

_____

_____

Do I feel like I am fighting the fact that I am divorced?

_____

_____

Am I angry with my ex-spouse?

_____

_____

Do I believe that deserve another chance from my ex-spouse?

_____

_____

Journaling

_____

_____

_____

_____

_____

_____

_____

_____

_____

_____

_____

_____

_____

_____

_____

_____

_____

_____

Journaling

Chapter Thirteen:

Working on Forgiveness

13 | Chapter Thirteen:
Working on Forgiveness

Reflection Questions:

What does true forgiveness mean to you?

_____

_____

_____

_____

_____

_____

_____

_____

_____

_____

_____

_____

_____

_____

Have you been able to forgive your spouse in this way, or at least entertain the idea?

_____

_____

_____

_____

_____

_____

_____

_____

_____

_____

_____

_____

_____

_____

_____

In addition to forgiving my spouse, are there other people I need to forgive?
Do I need to forgive myself for anything?

_____

_____

_____

_____

_____

_____

_____

_____

_____

_____

_____

_____

_____

_____

Now What?

Write down the action point you chose to use and the result of your action.

The point I chose to use was:

_____

_____

The result of my action was:

_____

_____

_____

_____

_____

_____

_____

Do I feel this helped me in my situation?

_____

_____

_____

_____

Implementation Questions

What are the benefits to the person who chooses to forgive?

_____

_____

_____

_____

_____

_____

_____

What are some concrete ways to begin or continue practicing forgiveness aside from what was mentioned previously?

_____

_____

_____

_____

_____

_____

Meditation Notes

_____

_____

_____

_____

_____

_____

_____

_____

Other Insights or Inspirations

_____

_____

_____

_____

_____

_____

Journaling

_____

_____

_____

_____

_____

_____

_____

_____

_____

_____

_____

_____

_____

_____

_____

_____

_____

Journaling

_____

_____

_____

_____

_____

_____

_____

_____

_____

_____

_____

_____

_____

_____

_____

_____

_____

Journaling

_____

_____

_____

_____

_____

_____

_____

_____

_____

_____

_____

_____

_____

_____

_____

_____

_____

_____

Chapter Fourteen:

Gratitude

14 | Chapter Fourteen: Gratitude

Reflection Questions:

We have seen many people endure suffering in their lives. Some carry their crosses with coldness and resentment; others with hope and peace. On a scale of 1 - 10 (10 being best) how would you rate your carrying of your cross of divorce?

_____

_____

_____

_____

_____

_____

_____

_____

_____

_____

_____

_____

Have you found it easy or difficult to identify blessings that you have received lately?

_____

_____

_____

_____

_____

_____

_____

_____

_____

_____

_____

_____

_____

_____

_____

_____

_____

When Simon of Cyrene helped Jesus carry his cross, he was angry at first for being coerced into the task. As he took that agonizing, slow trek with Christ through the city streets to Golgotha, the place of his execution, Simon's heart gradually softened and through carrying the cross, he came to know Jesus as his Savior. In contemplating this scene, do you find consolation in it? Why or why not?

_____

_____

_____

_____

_____

_____

_____

_____

_____

_____

_____

_____

_____

Now What?

Write down the action point you chose to use and the result of your action.

The point I chose to use was:

_____

_____

The result of my action was:

_____

_____

_____

_____

_____

_____

_____

Do I feel this helped me in my situation?

_____

_____

_____

_____

Implementation Questions

Name something you can be thankful that has come about as a result of your situation.

_____

_____

_____

_____

_____

_____

Do you pray for your spouse? Why or why not?

_____

_____

_____

_____

_____

_____

Meditation Notes

_____

_____

_____

_____

_____

_____

_____

_____

_____

Other Insights or Inspirations

_____

_____

_____

_____

_____

_____

_____

Things to Be Thankful For

Journaling

_____

_____

_____

_____

_____

_____

_____

_____

_____

_____

_____

_____

_____

_____

_____

_____

_____

Journaling

Chapter Fifteen:

Sex and Dating as a Divorced Catholic

15 | Chapter Fifteen:
Sex and Dating as a Divorced Catholic

Reflection Questions:

What has your opinion of dating become since your divorce or separation has taken place?

_____

_____

_____

_____

_____

_____

_____

_____

_____

_____

_____

_____

_____

_____

_____

_____

Are you feeling pressured by others to go out and date? How does this affect you?

If you have already dated since your divorce, describe your experiences.

_____

_____

_____

_____

_____

_____

_____

_____

_____

_____

_____

_____

_____

_____

_____

Now What?

Write down the action point you chose to use and the result of your action.

The point I chose to use was:

_____

_____

The result of my action was:

_____

_____

_____

_____

_____

_____

_____

_____

Do I feel this helped me in my situation?

_____

_____

_____

_____

Implementation Questions

If I am newly divorced or separated, how do I feel about spending the next year or more not dating, and if I have already been divorced for more than a year, what insights can I share about that period of time in my own experience?

_____

_____

_____

_____

_____

_____

Do I understand how "channeling" our energies works to help us stay in control of our bodies and our emotions?

_____

_____

_____

_____

_____

Meditation Notes

_____

_____

_____

_____

_____

_____

_____

_____

Other Insights or Inspirations

_____

_____

_____

_____

_____

_____

Journaling

_____

_____

_____

_____

_____

_____

_____

_____

_____

_____

_____

_____

_____

_____

_____

_____

_____

_____

Journaling

_____

_____

_____

_____

_____

_____

_____

_____

_____

_____

_____

_____

_____

_____

_____

_____

_____

_____

Journaling

_____

_____

_____

_____

_____

_____

_____

_____

_____

_____

_____

_____

_____

_____

_____

_____

Chapter Sixteen:

Mary, Our Mother

16 | Chapter Sixteen:
Mary, Our Mother

Reflection Questions:

How is your relationship with the Blessed Mother? Is she someone you
would consider looking to as a role model?

_____

_____

_____

_____

_____

_____

_____

_____

_____

_____

_____

_____

_____

Do you know anyone who has been a great example in your life such as Valerie in the story?

_____

_____

_____

_____

_____

_____

_____

_____

_____

_____

_____

_____

_____

_____

What are society's views and opinions of Mary as a role model?

_____

_____

_____

_____

_____

_____

_____

_____

_____

_____

_____

_____

_____

_____

_____

_____

Now What?

Write down the action point you chose to use and the result of your action.

The point I chose to use was:

_____

_____

The result of my action was:

_____

_____

_____

_____

_____

_____

_____

Do I feel this helped me in my situation?

_____

_____

_____

_____

Implementation Questions

In contemplating Mary's life, is there a virtue in particular that has impressed me most or draws me closer to her?

_____

_____

_____

_____

_____

_____

Have I ever had any "close encounters" with Mary?

_____

_____

_____

_____

_____

_____

Meditation Notes

_____

_____

_____

_____

_____

_____

_____

_____

Other Insights or Inspirations

_____

_____

_____

_____

_____

_____

Virtue Building Worksheet

Take some time to reflect on the areas in your life you struggle with; losing your patience on a regular basis, blaming others for your faults, over-eating or drinking too much, living a chaste life, being dishonest, even in little things, gossiping, etc. Everyone struggles with these things to some degree. Write down the three that you have the most difficulty dealing with:

Problem	Virtue

Next, refer to the list of virtues on page 226 of the book and select a virtue to counteract each problem you have listed. For example, if you struggle with blaming others, you would select the virtue of responsibility, authenticity, integrity, or truthfulness. If you struggle with gossiping, you would choose the virtue of prudence, kindness, caution, loyalty, or friendship. Write the virtue you choose down in the Virtue section across from the problem.

Next, think of how you will attain the virtue. What concrete steps can you take that will help you make this change? For example, if you want to work on stopping gossip you might decide to excuse yourself from a conversation that turns into gossip or instead of joining in the gossip, bring up some good points about the person in question and change the subject. Be sure to look at this list often, even every day, if possible. Feel free to post it on your refrigerator, mirror, etc.

Journaling

Journaling

Chapter Seventeen:

Hope for the Future and Our Vocation in Life

17 | Chapter Seventeen:
Hope for the Future and Our Vocation in Life

Reflection Questions:

What is your opinion about consulting God when it comes to major life decisions? Have you found this easy or difficult to do in the past?

_____

_____

_____

_____

_____

_____

_____

_____

_____

_____

_____

_____

_____

_____

_____

_____

_____

_____

_____

How about now? Do you find that you now seek God's counsel on decisions you have to make, regardless of how big or little?

_____

_____

_____

_____

_____

_____

_____

_____

_____

_____

_____

_____

_____

_____

_____

_____

_____

_____

_____

Now What?

Write down the action point you chose to use and the result of your action.

The point I chose to use was:

_____

_____

The result of my action was:

_____

_____

_____

_____

_____

_____

_____

_____

Do I feel this helped me in my situation?

_____

_____

_____

_____

Implementation Questions

Have I been aware of God's voice in my heart and how have I reacted?

_____

_____

_____

_____

_____

_____

Do I believe I have unique circumstances in my life or specific talents that I can share with others in a positive and inspirational way?

_____

_____

_____

_____

_____

_____

Meditation Notes

_____

_____

_____

_____

_____

_____

_____

_____

Other Insights or Inspirations

_____

_____

_____

_____

_____

_____

Journaling

Journaling

Journaling

Stations of the Cross
for those suffering through divorce or separation

Begin with the Sign of the Cross: In the name of the Father, and of the Son, and of the Holy Spirit. Amen.

Opening Scripture Reading

The Son of Man is destined to suffer grievously, to be rejected, and to be raised up on the third day. If anyone wants to be a follower of mine, let him renounce himself and take up his cross every day and follow me. For anyone who wants to save his life will lose it; but anyone who loses his life for my sake, that man will save it (*Luke* 9:22-24).

Opening Prayer

Lord Jesus, help me to be open to your closeness and presence as I begin this journey to Calvary with you. Help me to find in your Passion and Death the strength to take up my cross and follow you.

First Station:
Pilate Condemns Jesus to Die

I adore you, O Christ, and I praise you, because by your holy cross you have redeemed the world.

Meditation: Lord Jesus, often I feel unjustly judged by the court system, just as you were. At times even my friends and family voice their judgmental interpretation of my situation and fail to be understanding or loving. Help me to react as you did; with the quiet confidence of knowing that God our Father knows the truth. Help me to seek you as my most ardent Defender.

Be the source of my strength, that in you I will have strength for everything.

Our Father . . .   Hail Mary . . .   Glory Be . . .

Second Station:
Jesus Accepts His Cross

I adore you, O Christ, and I praise you, because by your holy cross you have redeemed the world.

Meditation: Lord Jesus, the cross that you willingly accepted was weighted down by our sins, for you are blameless and without sin. My cross is heavy too, Lord. My sins make it difficult to carry, but the weight placed on it by the person who hurt me most makes it seem unbearable to hold. When the weight of the cross of divorce overwhelms me Lord, prompt me to unite my sufferings to yours. Help me to remember the burden that you bore for my sake.

Be the source of my strength, that in you I will have strength for everything.

Our Father . . .   Hail Mary . . .   Glory Be . . .

Third Station:
Jesus Falls the First Time

I adore you, O Christ, and I praise you, because by your holy cross you have redeemed the world.

Meditation: Lord Jesus, over the years I have developed sinful patterns of behavior. These sinful choices coupled with my lack of focus and attention on you helped to create an environment void of peace. Through your mercy and grace, I've come to recognize the part I played in the breakup of my marriage. But patterns are hard to change, Lord. Please give me the grace not to fall back into those sinful patterns. And if I do, help me to remember your first fall. And fill me with the courage to get back up and begin again.

Be the source of my strength, that in you I will have strength for everything.

Our Father . . .   Hail Mary . . .   Glory Be . . .

Forth Station:
Jesus Meets His Mother

I adore you, O Christ, and I praise you, because by your holy cross you have redeemed the world.

<u>Meditation</u>: Lord Jesus, when you mother Mary's eyes met yours she was overcome by your suffering. Do I take the time to notice the suffering of others? Sometimes I fear that I am so consumed with my own suffering that I pay little or no attention to what others may be feeling. Open my eyes, Jesus to each opportunity that you provide for me to empathize with those around me. Teach me the true meaning of Humility, one of the greatest virtues of your Blessed Mother. Help me to understand that humility does not mean to think less of myself, but to think of myself *less*.

Be the source of my strength, that in you I will have strength for everything.

Our Father . . .   Hail Mary . . .   Glory Be . . .

Fifth Station:
Simon Helps Carry the Cross

I adore you, O Christ, and I praise you, because by your holy cross you have redeemed the world.

Meditation: Lord, Jesus in your humility you allowed Simon to help you with the burden of your cross. Many people have reached out to me also in an effort to relieve my suffering. Sometimes I find it so difficult to accept their help, Lord. I'd like to think that I can do it all by myself. I can't. Release me from my prideful tendencies. Help me to accept their help as you accepted the help of Simon.

Be the source of my strength, that in you I will have strength for everything.

Our Father . . .   Hail Mary . . .   Glory Be . . .

Sixth Station:
Veronica Wipes the Face of Jesus

I adore you, O Christ, and I praise you, because by your holy cross you have redeemed the world.

Meditation: As I meditate on this station it is easy to see Veronica's compassion for you in your time of sorrow. But what is important here is something more subtle and more powerful: even in the midst of your most painful suffering, you left your imprint on Veronica's cloth as well as her heart. Am I so consumed with being politically correct that I'm afraid to share my faith with others? Teach me, dear Lord, to find ways to leave your imprint on the people I meet today in spite of my hardships.

Be the source of my strength, that in you I will have strength for everything.

Our Father . . .   Hail Mary . . .   Glory Be . . .

Seventh Station:
Jesus Falls the Second Time

I adore you, O Christ, and I praise you, because by your holy cross you have redeemed the world.

Meditation: Placing myself at the scene of your second fall I can see the soldiers and the crowd laughing at your physical weakness. They make jokes at your expense and they enjoy seeing you fail. They call you names and proclaim you a fraud. I'm ashamed, Lord. How many times have I gotten satisfaction over the falls and failings of the one who has hurt me the most? Sometimes I just wait for some hardship to befall that person so I can publicly humiliate them. Heal my heart Lord. Help me not to repay evil for evil but instead teach me to forgive and forget.

Be the source of my strength, that in you I will have strength for everything.

Our Father . . .   Hail Mary . . .   Glory Be . . .

Eighth Station:
Jesus Speaks to the Women

I adore you, O Christ, and I praise you, because by your holy cross you have redeemed the world.

Meditation: This station used to puzzle me, Lord. I could not understand why you would tell these sorrowful women not to weep for you, but to weep for themselves and for their children. Now I see why. You could see, even then, all of the painful suffering that parents and children would go through when families fall apart. You especially had tremendous compassion and sorrow for the children. I'm so sorry Jesus for all of the pain this is causing my children. Surround them with their Guardian Angels and ask your Blessed Mother to wrap them within her loving mantle. Heal their hearts, Lord.

Be the source of my strength, that in you I will have strength for everything.

Our Father . . .   Hail Mary . . .   Glory Be . . .

Ninth Station:
Jesus Falls the Third Time

I adore you, O Christ, and I praise you, because by your holy cross you have redeemed the world.

Meditation: Lord, when I contemplate you falling for the third time it's hard to understand how you were able to go on. So many times I feel as though I can't go on. Just when I think that I've hit a stride another obstacle trips me up and I fall . . . again. Help me to see that when I am most vulnerable, when my heart is broken wide open and I think that my situation is hopeless that you desire my SURRENDER. I want to give it all to you, Jesus. Please teach me how. I cannot do this without you, Lord. Piece together my broken heart and spirit with the healing power of your love.

Be the source of my strength, that in you I will have strength for everything.

Our Father . . .   Hail Mary . . .   Glory Be . . .

Tenth Station:
Jesus is Stripped of His Garments

I adore you, O Christ, and I praise you, because by your holy cross you have redeemed the world.

Meditation: Lord Jesus, seeing you so cruelly humiliated as they intentionally stripped you of your garments grieves my heart. I offer up to you the many humiliations that I have suffered as a result of my divorce. Please strip me of all of my past embarrassments that this divorce has caused me. And clothe me with the virtues of your Blessed Mother: faithfulness, obedience, prudence, patience, mercy and purity.

Be the source of my strength, that in you I will have strength for everything.

Our Father . . .   Hail Mary . . .   Glory Be . . .

Eleventh Station:
Jesus is Nailed to the Cross

I adore you, O Christ, and I praise you, because by your holy cross you have redeemed the world.

Meditation: Christ, you lived in the truth and were nailed to a cross because of it. The crowd preferred to live in darkness surrounded by lies and fueled by hatred. I am so tired of living in darkness. I'm tired of all of the lies and hatred that swirl around me as I see my marriage fall apart. I am going to nail every lie to your cross and plead for the grace to live in the truth. I will no longer accept lies and deception in my life. You are the Way, the Truth and the Life, Jesus. Give me the courage that it takes to live an authentic life as you did.

Be the source of my strength, that in you I will have strength for everything.

Our Father . . .   Hail Mary . . .   Glory Be . . .

Twelfth Station:
Jesus Dies on the Cross

I adore you, O Christ, and I praise you, because by your holy cross you have redeemed the world.

Meditation: I give this moment to you, Jesus. Help me to think of nothing other that the fact that you died for ME. How can I turn my back on you now, Lord? So often I have taken the gift of my faith for granted; going to mass out of obligation and begrudgingly participating in the sacraments. I'm sorry, Jesus. I am reminded of the Roman soldier whose servant you so mercifully healed. From my heart I utter his prayer, "I believe. Help my unbelief." Help me to realize the richness and fullness of my Catholic Faith. Especially inspire me to desire you, who are fully present in the Eucharist.

Be the source of my strength, that in you I will have strength for everything.

Our Father . . .   Hail Mary . . .   Glory Be . . .

Thirteenth Station:
Jesus is Taken From the Cross

I adore you, O Christ, and I praise you, because by your holy cross you have redeemed the world.

Meditation: My heart breaks when I think of your mother's overwhelming loss. Your lifeless body was taken down from the cross and she lovingly held you in her arms. Jesus, I see the failure of my marriage as an overwhelming loss too. Please encourage me to rely on Mary's motherly love. Help me to place my loss into her loving arms. Open my heart to her consolation. Help me rely on her infinite desire to draw me closer to you, her son.

Be the source of my strength, that in you I will have strength for everything.

Our Father . . .   Hail Mary . . .   Glory Be . . .

Fourteenth Station:
Jesus is Laid in the Tomb

I adore you, O Christ, and I praise you, because by your holy cross you have redeemed the world.

Meditation: The tomb was such an empty and cold place for the King of Kings and the Lord of Lords to dwell, even in death. I reflect on my soul, where you also desire to dwell. Is it empty and cold too, Lord? In Your great mercy and love for us, Jesus, you have provided an opportunity to soften our hearts and make our souls warm and inviting to your presence: the sacrament of Reconciliation. I need your help to overcome my fear and weakness. Fill me with true contrition for my sins and a deep desire to begin again with the grace you pour down on me in this sacrament of love.

Be the source of my strength, that in you I will have strength for everything.

Our Father . . .   Hail Mary . . .   Glory Be . . .

Closing Scripture Reading

But at daybreak on the first day of the week they took the spices they had prepared and went to the tomb. They found the stone rolled away from the tomb; but when they entered, they did not find the body of the Lord Jesus. While they were puzzling over this, behold, two men in dazzling garments appeared to them. They were terrified and bowed their faces to the ground. They said to them, "Why do you seek the living one among the dead? He is not here, but he has been raised. Remember what he said to you while he was still in Galilee, that the Son of Man must be handed over to sinners and be crucified, and rise on the third day." And they remembered his words (*Luke* 24:1-8).

Closing Prayer

Lord Jesus, help me to walk with you each day of my life, even to Calvary. The sorrow and joy, the pain and healings, the failures and triumphs of my life are truly small deaths and resurrections that lead me to closeness with you. Give me the faith and trust I need to walk with you always. Amen.

Patron Saints
for those suffering through divorce or separation

St. Helen (249-329)

Helen's husband of 22 years divorced her to marry a woman who was a member of Rome's imperial family, which would put him in a politically advantageous position. St. Helen was also known for finding the True Cross in Jerusalem after Jesus' death.

St. Eugene de Mazenod (1782 - 1861)

Eugene was born into a very untraditional and turbulent family life. The only son of Charles and Marie-Rose, he experienced the pain and lonliness of divorce when his mother, who came from a wealthy family, divorced his father who came from a poor family and took back her dowry. After all was said and done, Marie-Rose wrote him a letter stating, "Now you have nothing." Despite this tragedy, Eugene went on to become a priest, and eventually the Bishop of Marsailles, France in 1837. He also founded the Oblates of Mary Immaculate in 1826.

St. Joseph, Foster Father of Jesus

Joseph was a great man; full of integrity and compassion. He and Mary were betrothed when he discovered Mary was pregnant, and the problem for him, then, was the child was not his. For this reason, he planned to divorce Mary according to the law. He was as yet unaware that she was carrying the Son of God. Being the good man that he was, he was concerned for her suffering and safety, for in those days, women accused of adultery could be stoned to death, so he decided to divorce her quietly and not expose her to shame or cruelty (Matthew 1:19-25).

Because Joseph had a great faith, he was certainly obedient to whatever God asked of him, even though he did not quite understand what would happen as a result. When Joseph was asleep and the Angel appeared to him in a dream, he was told the true story about Mary and the child she was carrying. Without hesitation, Joseph immediately took Mary as his wife. Joseph reacted in the same manner when the angel came again to alert him to the danger that waited for his family. He immediately left everything and fled to a strange country with his family where he waited until the angel told him it was safe to go back (Matthew 2:13-23).

Excellent Prayers
Memorare to the Blessed Mother

Remember, O most gracious Virgin Mary, that never was it known, that anyone who fled to your protection, implored your help, or sought your intercession was left unaided. Inspired by this confidence, I fly unto you, O Virgin of virgins, my Mother. To you I come, before you I stand, sinful and sorrowful. O Mother of the Word Incarnate, despise not my petition but in your mercy, hear and answer me. Amen.

Memorare to Saint Joseph

Remember, most pure spouse of Mary ever Virgin, my loving protector St. Joseph, that never has it been heard that anyone invoked your protection or besought your aid without being consoled. In this confidence I come before you; I fervently recommend myself to you. Despise not my prayer, foster father of the Redeemer, but graciously deign to hear it. Amen.

An Act of Faith

My God, I firmly believe that you are the one God in three divine Persons: Father, Son and Holy Spirit. I believe that your divine Son became man and died for our sins, and that he will come to judge the living and the dead. I believe these and all the truths that the holy Catholic Church teaches, because you revealed them, who can neither deceive, nor be deceived.

An Act of Hope

My God, relying on your infinite goodness and promises, I hope to obtain pardon of my sins, the help of your grace, and life everlasting, through the merits of Jesus Christ, my Lord and Redeemer. Lord, may I be happy with you forever. Amen.

Act of Charity

My God, I love you with all my heart above all else, because you are infinitely good and our everlasting happiness. Out of love for you, I love my neighbor as myself and I forgive anyone who has hurt me. Lord, enable me to love you more and more. Amen.

Chaplet of Divine Mercy
Recited using rosary beads

1. Begin with the Sign of the Cross, and then recite one Our Father, one Hail Mary and The Apostles Creed.

2. On the Our Father Beads say the following:

   Eternal Father, I offer You the Body and Blood, Soul and Divinity of Your dearly beloved Son, Our Lord Jesus Christ, in atonement for our sins and those of the whole world.

3. On the 10 Hail Mary Beads say the following:

   For the sake of His sorrowful Passion, have mercy on us and on the whole world.

   (Repeat step 2 and 3 for all five decades).

4. Conclude with (three times):

   Holy God, Holy Mighty One, Holy Immortal One, have mercy on us and on the whole world.

Stay With Me
Daily Prayer of St. Padre Pio

Stay with me, Lord, for it is necessary to have You present so that I do not forget You. You know how easily I abandon You.

Stay with me, Lord, because I am weak and I need Your strength, that I may not fall so often.

Stay with me, Lord, for You are my life, and without You, I am without fervor.

Stay with me, Lord, for You are my light, and without You, I am in darkness.

Stay with me, Lord, to show me Your will.

Stay with me, Lord, so that I hear Your voice and follow You.

Stay with me, Lord, for I desire to love You very much, and always be in Your company.

Stay with me, Lord, if You wish me to be faithful to You.

Stay with me, Lord, for as poor as my soul is, I want it to be a place of consolation for You, a nest of love.

Stay with me, Jesus, for it is getting late and the day is coming to a close, and life passes; death, judgment, eternity approaches. It is necessary to renew my strength, so that I will not stop along the way and for that, I need You. It is getting late and death approaches, I fear the darkness, the temptations, the dryness, the cross, the sorrows. O how I need You, my Jesus, in this night of exile!

Stay with me tonight, Jesus, in life with all it's dangers. I need You. Let me recognize You as Your disciples did at the breaking of the bread, so that the Eucharistic Communion be the Light which disperses the darkness, the force which sustains me, the unique joy of my heart.

Stay with me, Lord, because at the hour of my death, I want to remain united to You, if not by communion, at least by grace and love.

Stay with me, Jesus, I do not ask for divine consolation, because I do not merit it, but the gift of Your Presence, oh yes, I ask this of You!

Stay with me, Lord, for it is You alone I look for, Your Love, Your Grace, Your Will, Your Heart, Your Spirit because I love You and ask no other reward but to love You more and more. With a firm love, I will love You with all my heart while on earth and continue to love You perfectly during all eternity. Amen.

How to Pray the Rosary

Make the Sign of the Cross and say the "Apostles' Creed."
Say the "Our Father."
Say three "Hail Marys."
Say the "Glory be to the Father."

Announce the First Mystery; then say the "Our Father."
Say ten "Hail Marys," while meditating on the Mystery.
Say the "Glory be to the Father."

Announce the Second Mystery; then say the "Our Father." Repeat 6 and 7 and continue with Third, Fourth and Fifth Mysteries in the same manner.

After the Rosary:

Hail, Holy Queen, Mother of Mercy, our life, our sweetness and our hope! To thee do we cry, poor banished children of Eve; to thee do we send up our sighs, mourning and weeping in this valley of tears. Turn then, most gracious advocate, thine eyes of mercy toward us, and after this our exile, show unto us the blessed fruit of thy womb, Jesus.
O clement, O loving, O sweet Virgin Mary!
Pray for us, O Holy Mother of God.
That we may be made worthy of the promises of Christ.

The Joyful mysteries are recited on Mondays and Saturdays, the Luminous mysteries on Thursdays, the Sorrowful mysteries on Tuesdays and Fridays, and the Glorious mysteries on Wednesdays and Sundays.